The Breakup Diary
Lisa Goich-Andreadis

Cover Art: Woman With Broken Heart/Paul Gilligan/Getty Images
Artville Collection

"The Breakup Diary." ISBN 1-58939-260-4 (softcover version).

Published 2002 by Virtualbookworm.com Publishing Inc., P.O. Box 9949, College Station, TX , 77842, US. ©2002 Lisa Goich-Andreadis. All rights reserved. No part of this publication may be reproduced, stored in a retrieval system, or transmitted in any form or by any means, electronic, mechanical, recording or otherwise, without the prior written permission of Lisa Goich-Andreadis.

Manufactured in the United States of America.

*To all the boys I've loved before
(and you know who you are!)*

xo

Thank You...

Mother and Father for always believing in me and encouraging me regardless of what silly venture I decided to get myself into.

Norm Stultz and Marty Whitsitt (and the bartender at the Oregon Express) who lent their ears and hearts to me during that tear-filled weekend in Dayton, Ohio so many years ago when this book was conceived.

Sara and Nicole for being the best nieces in the world. I hope this is a book you'll never need.

Richard, Kristina, Kathy, Darrell, Diva Tina, Christian, Auntie Dee, Uncle Mike, Cousin Karen, Bob, Fred, Jim, Sue and kids – I'm so fortunate to have a family filled with all of you!

All of my girlfriends who have been with me through all of the assorted heartbreaks throughout the years: Melanie, Connie, Donna, Diane, Kimmie and Mary Kay. McNutley, Ann, Tacky Jacky, Jackie Wo & Jill. Without all of you, I'd be cowering in a corner somewhere, still trying to get over Rich or Brad or Jim or Dale or Joel or...
A special thank you to Chato – an extraordinary writer, teacher and friend. Thank you to "The Cul de Sac" – the best place to live in the world.

Ollie, Lulu, Bowie, Zeke and Katy for giving me unconditional love every day.

And finally, last but certainly not least, Teddy – my husband, boyfriend and best buddy. You rescued me from Breakup World, and for that I am forever grateful.

I love you all.

Table of Contents

Introduction
Chapter 1   A Friend In Need
Chapter 2   Once More With Feeling
Chapter 3   Who, What, Where, When, *Whyyyy?*
Chapter 4   And Another Thing!
Chapter 5   The Best of Times, The Worst of Times
Chapter 6   Dear John
Chapter 7   Make Your Own Voodoo Doll!
Chapter 8   Good Things That Happened Today
Chapter 9   Don't Just Sit There...Do Something!
Chapter 10 I Think There's Something You Should Know
Chapter 11 Things That Make Your Stomach Go *Ughhh*!
Chapter 12 I *Swear* I'll Never Do It Again!
Chapter 13 There Is No Chapter 13!
Chapter 14 The Man Of Your Dreams
Chapter 15 To All The Boys You've Loved Before
Chapter 16 Stupid Things I've Done After A Breakup
Chapter 17 Promises, Promises
Chapter 18 Thank You Notes
Chapter 19 Yadda, Yadda, Yadda!
Chapter 20 Sweet REVENGE!
Chapter 21 I'm Cute Enough, I'm Smart Enough
Chapter 22 Kiss & Tell
Chapter 23 And Now, A Word About Love
Chapter 24 Roses Are Red
Chapter 25 Design Your Perfect Mate
Chapter 26 And If You're Still Not Feeling Better
Certificate Breakup Survival Certificate

Introduction

So you were dumped? It feels pretty crummy, doesn't it? When you're not staring at the ceiling listening to Alanis Morisette wondering what went wrong, you're reliving the moment with just about anyone who will listen: your girlfriends, your parents, your co-workers, the guy behind the counter at 7-Eleven, right?

Well, now that you've gotten the sympathy you so desperately needed (and a free giant soda if you were lucky), it's time for a little self-reflection. And self-reflection is what *The Breakup Diary* is all about.

The Breakup Diary is for anyone who is smack-dab in the middle of that icky, awful, feels-like-someone-punched-you-in-the-stomach, miserably lonely time that follows the loss of a love. And chances are if you've read this far, *The Breakup Diary* is for you!

This isn't a book. It's a guided journal. And because your attention span isn't quite what it normally is, I've kept the copy short, sweet and to the point. Because it's *your* thoughts that this book is about, not mine or anyone else's.

When working through *The Breakup Diary*, please feel free to bounce around between chapters. Though they're laid out in what I felt was a logical order, your needs may be different than my vision. So do what you need to do when you feel like doing it. *The Breakup Diary* gives you the freedom to express your feelings as you please.

Remember, where there's life there's hope. Here's hoping *The Breakup Diary* brings you a happily-ever-after ending of your own! Good luck!

- Lisa Goich-Andreadis

Lisa Goich-Andreadis

The movie Fatal Attraction really ruined things for women. You can't even call a guy 150 times a day anymore without having him get all bent out of shape!

1.
A Friend In Need

One can never make *too* many calls to their friends and relatives after a breakup. Well, okay...maybe they can. But that's what friends are for, right? Heck, if you can't cash your friendship tokens in after a horrific breakup, when can you cash them in? This chapter is a place for you to write down all of your friends and family members you can call 24-hours a day, no questions asked. After all, a friend in need is definitely a friend, indeed.

Name_____
Number_____

Name_____
Number_____

Name_____
Number_____

Name_____
Number_____

Name_____
Number_____

Name_____
Number_____

Name_____
Number_____

2.

Once More, With Feeling

How do you feel today? What would make you feel better right now? How do you hope to feel in six months from now? Here's a place to express your feelings in any way you wish – write them, draw them, paint them or record them on a tape recorder. Just be sure to date each entry so you can look back in a month from now and see all of the progress you've made!

_____

_____

_____

_____

_____

_____

_____

_____

_____

_____

_____

_____

_____

_____

_____

_____

_____

Lisa Goich-Andreadis

The Breakup Diary

Lisa Goich-Andreadis

The Breakup Diary

Lisa Goich-Andreadis

The Breakup Diary

Lisa Goich-Andreadis

The Breakup Diary

Lisa Goich-Andreadis

The Breakup Diary

Lisa Goich-Andreadis

The Breakup Diary

Feel Better Yet?

3.

Who, What, Where, When, Whyyyy?

Perhaps Nancy Kerrigan put it best after being slammed in the knee a few years ago when she said… "*Whyyyyyy?????*" In your case, it's "Why did you do it?" "Are you seeing someone else?" "What could I have done differently that would have made you stay?" "When will this awful feeling in my stomach go away?" Pulling all of the horrible questions from your heart – and writing them down on this page – will provide a happy alternative to unnecessary phone calls to your Ex. Rather than ask him the questions, ask the diary. Chances are, you'll come up with the same answers anyway. And *without* the humiliation!

Question away!

_____
_____
_____
_____
_____
_____
_____
_____
_____
_____
_____
_____
_____

Lisa Goich-Andreadis

Lisa Goich-Andreadis

Lisa Goich-Andreadis

The Breakup Diary

Lisa Goich-Andreadis

Lisa Goich-Andreadis

Lisa Goich-Andreadis

My last boyfriend broke up with me because he said I was psychotic! I said, "That's not true! I have never once predicted something before it happened!"

4.

And Another Thing!

In this chapter, you're encouraged to get out the ax and start whacking away at the pedestal you've so expertly placed your Ex upon since the big breakup. What are some of the things he did that really bugged you? What were some of his annoying habits that you overlooked because you *thought* you were in L-O-V-E? The purpose of this chapter is to help you realize that Mr. Thought-He-Was-Right, wasn't really that perfect, after all. He was merely a convenience to help you bide your time until the *real* Mr. Right comes along!

_____
_____
_____
_____
_____
_____
_____
_____
_____
_____
_____
_____
_____
_____
_____
_____

Lisa Goich-Andreadis

The Breakup Diary

Lisa Goich-Andreadis

The Breakup Diary

Lisa Goich-Andreadis

The Breakup Diary

Lisa Goich-Andreadis

The Breakup Diary

Lisa Goich-Andreadis

5.

The Best Of Times...The Worst Of Times

List five of the greatest moments you remember having with your ex:

-
-
-
-
-

OK, now list five times your ex made you so angry you almost left him:

-
-
-
-
-

Can you list five more?

-
-
-
-
-

See, he wasn't as great as you thought he was!

6.

Dear John

So it's 2 o'clock in the morning. You've been staring at the phone for five hours. It rang twice and both were hang-up calls. You tried to *69 the call, but the number was blocked. Darn! It could have been him. Hmmm...wonder if it was? Should you call him? No. You can't. How about writing him a letter? Not a letter to send! We *never* send letters after a breakup! Just a letter to keep in this Diary. In fact, there are plenty of pages provided in this section to write a letter whenever you *think* you need to talk to your Ex. There's nothing you need to say to him that can't be dumped here, or on your girlfriends (see chapter 1). So go ahead, write that letter. Then close the book and go to bed. You'll have nothing to regret in the morning!

_____

_____

_____

_____

_____

_____

_____

_____

_____

_____

_____

_____

_____

_____

The Breakup Diary

The Breakup Diary

Lisa Goich-Andreadis

The Breakup Diary

Lisa Goich-Andreadis

The Breakup Diary

Lisa Goich-Andreadis

Lisa Goich-Andreadis

Lisa Goich-Andreadis

Lisa Goich-Andreadis

Lisa Goich-Andreadis

The Breakup Diary

Lisa Goich-Andreadis

The Breakup Diary

Lisa Goich-Andreadis

I'd like to be a fish fly. It's a bug that only lives one day. They're born, they mate, they die. Kind of takes all the worry out of, "Will he ever call me again?"

7.

Make Your Own Voodoo Doll!

It's time to make your own Voodoo Doll! That's right, your own personalized Ex on paper that you can poke and prod and put hexes on all day long!

In the space provided on the following page, draw a picture of your Ex. It can be a stick figure, a silhouette or, if you're a Rembrandt-In-Training, go all out with a detailed portrait. You can even cut and paste an actual photo of your Ex!

Now for the fun part; if you could cast a hex on any part of his body, which part would it be? His hair, so it would all fall out? His ears that wouldn't listen to you the last time you called him? How about his smelly feet he used to put on your coffee table, which drove you totally crazy? Don't want him to look at another woman as long as he lives? You have the power to stop him in his tracks! Simply get out a push pin and start punching away! Next to each pinhole, write what you were feeling when you did it. Happy? Sad? Were you laughing hysterically? Even if you don't believe in evil spells and voodoo, you'll feel a lot better when you're done with this exercise. You can even cut him out at the end and hang him up on your bulletin board or refrigerator for a souvenir!

Now, let's get ready to HEX THE EX!

Lisa Goich-Andreadis

8.

Good Things That Happened Today

Accentuate the positive. Sweep the negative under the rug. It's a simple concept that works every time. Every day, for the next three months, you're to list all of the good things that happened to you. Nothing is too small or trite to write down. Got a call from an old friend? Did someone let you cut in front of him or her in traffic today? Did a handsome man hold the door open for you on your way in to work this morning? Don't spare yourself the joy of these delicious little moments.

Start writing!

_____
_____
_____
_____
_____
_____
_____
_____
_____
_____
_____
_____

Lisa Goich-Andreadis

The Breakup Diary

Lisa Goich-Andreadis

The Breakup Diary

Lisa Goich-Andreadis

The Breakup Diary

Lisa Goich-Andreadis

The Breakup Diary

Lisa Goich-Andreadis

9.

Don't Just Sit There...*Do Something!*

Unless you have a particularly handsome mailman, good-looking men or interesting people aren't going to be knocking on your door every day. You're going to have to get up off your butt and go find *them!* Every day you have to write down one activity in this chapter and *do it!* Whether it's an afternoon at the bookstore or a trip to the water park with a niece or nephew, the simple act of breaking up the monotonous work/home/work schedule with a little fun can do *wonders* for a weary heart (not to mention what it can do for the ol' love life!). Now get out there and *do something!*

Lisa Goich-Andreadis

The Breakup Diary

Lisa Goich-Andreadis

Lisa Goich-Andreadis

The Breakup Diary

Lisa Goich-Andreadis

The Breakup Diary

Lisa Goich-Andreadis

I hate when brides-to-be make their single girlfriends look at bridal magazines. I think that's just plain RUDE! Making a single woman look at a bridal magazine is like making a homeless man look at a copy of Architectural Digest. "See this triple-tiered oak deck with the marble fountain in the center? You'll never set foot on anything like this in your entire life!"

10.

I Think There's Something You Should Know

Frequently after the breakup – like at *least* once every day – you're going to find yourself digging for excuses to call your Ex. Mostly to tell him insignificant things that happened during the day, which at one time he *might* have been interested in. Problem is, he's not interested any more. To break yourself of the habit (and to save yourself a lot of humiliation) use this chapter to record all of those daily "newsflashes" you're just itchin' to tell your Ex. It'll do wonders for your pride, not to mention your phone bill!

_____
_____
_____
_____
_____
_____
_____
_____
_____
_____
_____
_____
_____
_____
_____

The Breakup Diary

The Breakup Diary

Lisa Goich-Andreadis

The Breakup Diary

Lisa Goich-Andreadis

The Breakup Diary

Lisa Goich-Andreadis

The Breakup Diary

11.

Things That Make Your Stomach Go *Ughhh!*

After a breakup or divorce, thoughts of your Ex have a way of making their way into your mind, crawling down into your heart then taking a nose-dive straight into your stomach. This is the chapter to jot down all of those thoughts as they pop into your mind. Whether it's that song heard on the radio that stirred up memories of your Ex, or the car you spotted a thousand times today that looked *just like his*, all of those tummy-turning things should be stopped dead in their tracks, and recorded right here.

_____
_____
_____
_____
_____
_____
_____
_____
_____
_____
_____
_____
_____
_____
_____
_____

The Breakup Diary

Lisa Goich-Andreadis

The Breakup Diary

Lisa Goich-Andreadis

The Breakup Diary

Lisa Goich-Andreadis

The Breakup Diary

Lisa Goich-Andreadis

The Breakup Diary

12.

I *Swear* I'll Never Do It Again!

Whether it's a certain type of person to avoid, or a specific habit you seem to repeat over and over again, this is the chapter of the book to reflect upon and record these "mistakes." Hopefully, as you become aware of them, you won't repeat them in your next relationship. And *yes*, there will be a "next" relationship!

_____
_____
_____
_____
_____
_____
_____
_____
_____
_____
_____
_____
_____
_____
_____
_____
_____
_____
_____
_____

The Breakup Diary

Lisa Goich-Andreadis

The Breakup Diary

Lisa Goich-Andreadis

The answering machine can be quite a dangerous piece of equipment in a relationship. One night, when my Ex and I came home from dinner, he went into his office to check his answering machine. From the other room I could very faintly hear a woman's voice babbling on and on and on saying, "Hi Dale. I miss you. I was hoping we could get together tonight for dinner or something." I couldn't take it anymore. I leapt up from the couch, ran into his office and said,
"Who in the &*$#%... oh... it's me. Never mind!"

13.

There Is No Chapter 13...
You've Had Enough Bad Luck Already!

Now move along...

14.

The Man Of Your Dreams

After a breakup, closing your eyes at night can be a pretty scary thing. You just *know* you're going to have another dream about your Ex. Waking up in the morning can leave you wanting more – and that's just not a safe place for you to be in at this point. But have no fear, there's a way you can use those dreams to help you work through the breakup. For instance, if you find yourself dreaming about your Ex and other women, you'll actually find that if you ever *do* see him with someone else, it's going to make it a lot easier because you've been through it again and again in dreamland! So write down those dreams, and let *them* help *you* get over *him*!

_____
_____
_____
_____
_____
_____
_____
_____
_____
_____
_____
_____
_____
_____
_____
_____

Lisa Goich-Andreadis

Lisa Goich-Andreadis

The Breakup Diary

Lisa Goich-Andreadis

The Breakup Diary

Lisa Goich-Andreadis

Lisa Goich-Andreadis

The Breakup Diary

Lisa Goich-Andreadis

The Breakup Diary

Lisa Goich-Andreadis

The Breakup Diary

15.

To All The Boys You've Loved Before

Love was easy when you were a kid. All you had to do was tell your girlfriend you "liked" somebody and – less than 24-hours later – you'd be "going together!" Ahhh, the good ol' days! In this chapter of the book, we're going to go back to those days and have you recall things like:

- Who was your first boyfriend?

- Why did you like him?

- Who dumped who?

- How did you feel at the time?

- How long did it take you to get over it?

- Now list the three major loves of your life and the reason the relationships ended:

- Now name one good thing that came out of each one of those relationships.

- Now name one good thing that came out of each one of those breakups.

See, you've loved before, you've gotten over it, you WILL do it again!

The Breakup Diary

This is a poem I wrote to my sixth-grade boyfriend Shawn after he broke up with me:

I've loved you now for many a day
But my feelings are only rejected
I know that even a glance from you
Is too much to be expected.

I'm much too blind to see the light
To see you don't care for me
Instead I sit back playing the fool
Waiting for what won't be.

When my sense and my strength both build
And I gain back my long-lost pride
I'll realize that my feelings for you
Have not grown but only died!

(Pretty *deeeeep* for an 11-year-old!)

16.

Stupid Things I've Done After A Breakup

I once bought a magic wand from a woman who said I could wave it over my head to make myself "more desirable" to the opposite sex. During a *waving* one day, the Rose Quartz stone on the end of the wand fell off and hit me in the forehead leaving me with a knot that just looked like a large zit...very desirable!

- I drove by my Ex's house with a friend one day and ducked down in my seat so he wouldn't see me. The problem was, *I* was driving the car! I ran into a fire hydrant at the end of the street and put a nasty dent on my car! Thank goodness he wasn't home at the time. How embarrassing would THAT have been?????

How many stupid things have YOU done?

17.

Promises, Promises

What empty promises did your Ex fill the air with when you were together? "I promise to take care of you always"? "I promise that we will be together forever"? "I promise that I'll never hurt you"? Yuck! Makes you want to scream just thinking about it, doesn't it? The space below is the perfect canvas to paint these empty promises on. When you're finished you should be able to clearly see that he wasn't the prince he appeared to be, after all.

_____
_____
_____
_____
_____
_____
_____
_____
_____
_____
_____
_____
_____
_____
_____
_____

Lisa Goich-Andreadis

The Breakup Diary

Lisa Goich-Andreadis

The Breakup Diary

18.

Thank You Notes

What are you thankful for today? Your family? Your job? Your dogs? The fact that God gave you a really good butt? Not a day should go by without placing an entry in this chapter. In the end, you'll realize how truly blessed you are! Now go ahead, get grateful!

_____
_____
_____
_____
_____
_____
_____
_____
_____
_____
_____
_____
_____
_____
_____
_____
_____
_____
_____
_____
_____
_____

The Breakup Diary

Lisa Goich-Andreadis

The Breakup Diary

Lisa Goich-Andreadis

19.

Yadda, Yadda, Yadda

After a breakup, friends and family members are full of trite clichés that they think will help you get over your lost relationship. Things like, "There are plenty of fish in the sea," and "If it was meant to be, it will be." Use this chapter to record all of these sayings and words of advice. Oddly enough, after reading through them, you just might realize that they were "right on the money." And instead of "crying over spilt milk," and "throwing in the towel," you should just "roll with the punches" and "let bygones be bygones." OK. Your turn.

Lisa Goich-Andreadis

The Breakup Diary

Lisa Goich-Andreadis

The Breakup Diary

It's no wonder women and men don't get along. We're completely different. Even our speech patterns aren't the same. I read somewhere that women speak 45 thousand words a day and men speak 18 thousand. That's a big difference! But when you think about it, it's absolutely true. Here's an example. Woman and man sit down to dinner after work one day. Woman says to the man, "So honey, how was your day at work today?" The man says, "Fine." That's 9-to-1 right there! And it continues all day long. "What do you want to watch on TV tonight?" "Whatever." "Did you talk to John today? How's John doing?" "OK." And it continues even in the bedroom. The woman says, "I love you so much honey. Let's just cuddle and talk, cuddle and talk. Let's talk about today, talk about tomorrow, talk about yesterday... talk, talk, talk." The man says, "Yeah honey, I love you t... snoreeeeee" And you thought he fell asleep? He didn't fall asleep! He just ran out of his words for the day!

20.

Sweet Revenge!

Okay. It's time to get a little nasty. Use the space below to list all of the not-so-fortunate things you wish would befall your Ex. Be spontaneous, and simply list the first things that come to your mind, no matter how silly you think they are. It can be anything from "I wish he would go bald," to "I wish he would fall in love with a beautiful woman only to find out – in the heat of passion – that the woman is really a *man*." Have fun and don't hold back. Let 'er rip!

Lisa Goich-Andreadis

The Breakup Diary

Lisa Goich-Andreadis

The Breakup Diary

21.

I'm Cute Enough, I'm Smart Enough

So your Ex left you feeling pretty crummy, huh? Well, it's time to stop dwelling on him and the state of mind he's put you in, and start paying attention to all of those wonderful things everyone else is saying about you. Things you've been just too gosh-darned downtrodden to hear. "You're better off without him." "He was lucky to have you." "You're so pretty, you'll find a new guy in no time!" Any of these sound familiar? How about writing down a few of your own?

_____
_____
_____
_____
_____
_____
_____
_____
_____
_____
_____
_____
_____
_____
_____
_____
_____
_____

The Breakup Diary

Lisa Goich-Andreadis

The Breakup Diary

Lisa Goich-Andreadis

22.

Kiss & Tell

Quick! Name five FAMOUS people you could picture yourself kissing! Now, name five people in your life right now you wouldn't mind getting to know a little better. Keep going! The easier it is for you to picture yourself with other guys, the easier it'll actually be to do it when the opportunity presents itself. How about that guy in your yoga class? The UPS man? That cute guy in your office? Love will be here again sooner than you think!

Lisa Goich-Andreadis

The Breakup Diary

Lisa Goich-Andreadis

The Breakup Diary

Lisa Goich-Andreadis

*I'm dating a guy who's 21.
That's 7 in boy years!*

23.

And Now, A Word About Love

This is a section for you to write down some of your favorite quotes, song lyrics, poems and thoughts about love. When you're finished, you'll find you've amassed a nice collection you'll want to refer to again and again!

Lisa Goich-Andreadis

The Breakup Diary

Lisa Goich-Andreadis

The Breakup Diary

The Breakup Diary

Lisa Goich-Andreadis

The Breakup Diary

Lisa Goich-Andreadis

24.

Roses Are Red

It's time to GET CREATIVE! Write a poem, draw a picture, let the creativity flow! Use markers, pens, pencils, glitter or glue. Cut pictures out of magazines. Take a photo of your Ex, cut out his head and replace it with someone else's. Just have fun! This is the section of the book to get wild and do whatever you please!

Lisa Goich-Andreadis

Get Creative!

The Breakup Diary

Get Creative!

25.

Design Your Perfect Mate

Ready to think about the *New & Improved* man of your dreams? The future "Mr. Right?" There's no better time to start planning for tomorrow than right now. In the days of designer babies and cloned sheep, wouldn't it be GREAT if you could design your perfect mate? Well, now's your chance! What do you picture him looking like? A blonde or brunette? Short or tall? Doctor or football player? Sporty or couch potato? Today's dreams are tomorrow's reality. Start designing!

Eyes _____

Hair _____

Height _____

Weight _____

Background _____

Nationality _____

Profession _____

Personality _____

Hobbies _____

Other _____

I've known from the time I was a child that I wouldn't be married. Remember that song The Farmer In The Dell? Whenever it got to the part, "...a farmer takes a wife..." nobody ever picked me. I was always the cheese!

26.

And if You're Still Not Feeling Better

Use the next few pages to jot down any books, tapes, CDs or websites you run across yourself or have suggested to you by friends. There's nothing like getting absorbed in a great movie or novel to help you forget about your Ex!

_____
_____
_____
_____
_____
_____
_____
_____
_____
_____
_____
_____
_____
_____
_____
_____
_____
_____
_____

The Breakup Diary

Lisa Goich-Andreadis

The Breakup Diary

Lisa Goich-Andreadis

The "I-Survived-A-Breakup-And-All-I-Got-Was-This-Lousy-Certificate" Certificate

Congratulations!

You're officially OVER HIM! Aren't you proud of yourself? We knew you could do it!

To commemorate this monumental event, you deserve something special! How about a FREE COPY of the *I-Survived-A-Breakup-And-All-I-Got-Was-This-Lousy-Certificate* Certificate? To redeem your certificate, simply write to:

Certificate
BreakupDiary@aol.com

Include your name, address, city, state, zip and e-mail address with your request. You'll receive your certificate in 4-6 weeks. We'll also keep you posted on any *Breakup Diary* events in your area.

Meanwhile, if you need future support, a cyber-shoulder to cry on or just want to share your story with other people who are feeling just like you are, visit us at www.breakupdiary.com. We're there for you 24-hours a day! In fact, you might want to add us to your "Friend In Need" list in Chapter 1!

Now what are you waiting for? Get out there and have some fun. There's a future Mr. Right wandering around out there just waiting to be discovered.

Go get 'em!

Lisa Goich-Andreadis

I had a boyfriend once who broke up with me for snooping. I said, I don't like to think of it as snooping. I like to think of it as Investigative Cleaning!

The Beginning...

About The Author

Lisa Goich-Andreadis is a stand-up comedian, talk radio host, award-winning copywriter, lover of all things four-legged and recovering "Breakupee." She currently lives in Los Angeles with her husband Teddy and five furry children. *The Breakup Diary* is her first published work.

The Breakup Diary

Printed in the United States
1504200005B/256